SIX OR TV
OR INDIVIC

FOUNDATIONS I

Basic Blocks for Building a Life of Faith

John Cervone & Arnold Fleagle

● ● ● ● ● ● ● ● ● ● ● ● ● ● ● ● ● ● ● ●

Christian Publications

CAMP HILL, PENNSYLVANIA

Walking with the Word
Bible Studies

Christian Publications, Inc.
3825 Hartzdale Drive, Camp Hill, PA 17011

Faithful, Biblical Publishing Since 1883

ISBN: 0-87509-684-0
© 1997 by Christian Publications, Inc.
All rights reserved
Printed in the United States of America

97 98 99 00 01   5 4 3 2 1

Unless otherwise indicated, Scripture taken from the HOLY BIBLE: NEW INTERNATIONAL VERSION ®. © 1973, 1978, 1984 by the International Bible Society. Used by permission of Zondervan Publishing House. All rights reserved.

CONTENTS

Introduction	**5**
1 The Assurance of Salvation	**7**
2 Studying the Scriptures	**13**
3 Prayer	**19**
4 Witnessing	**27**
5 Worship and Fellowship	**35**
6 Stewardship	**43**
Leader's Guide	**49**

Introduction

The most significant decision anyone can ever make is to decide to follow Jesus Christ as Savior and Lord. *Foundations* is a course of study that has been designed to build up your faith—to help you gain a firm foundation and grow in spiritual maturity.

Jesus tells us that our faith—what we believe and how we live—is like the wise man who builds his house upon the rock. When the winds of trouble come and beat against the house, it will stand (see Matthew 7:24-27).

Foundations is designed to be used in Sunday school classes, small groups or individual study. It contains six lessons. You may choose to do one lesson a week or spend two weeks on each lesson.

The *Leader's Guide,* which begins on page 49, provides answers to most questions and additional background material to assist you in your study.

Our prayer for you is that your faith will grow as you follow Jesus Christ and permit Him to be Lord of every facet of your life.

We readily recognize David Fessenden of Christian Publications who assisted us in creating the

6 INTRODUCTION

proper format to present this series of studies. Also, we are grateful for the many hours of labor that were invested by Gail Roso, our church secretary at Stow Alliance Fellowship.

By His grace,
John C. Cervone and Arnold R. Fleagle

STUDY ONE

The Assurance of Salvation

You are standing at one end of a high bridge which crosses a raging river. Your friends are waving and shouting at you to cross the bridge and join them. As you attempt the crossing, which situation would you rather face—strong faith in a weak bridge or weak faith in a strong bridge? Strong faith in a weak bridge will land you in the river, but weak faith in a strong bridge will land you on the other side! Faith is only as valuable as its object.

The assurance of your salvation is grounded in the person of Jesus Christ and the promises of God's Word. Robert Cook wrote, "Salvation is not something you do, but something Christ does when you receive Him."[1]

It is inevitable that doubts will come to you about the reality of your salvation, but they will vanish like the early morning fog in the noonday sun if you focus on God's Word and the fact of Jesus' death and resurrection. Your salvation is a fact regardless of your moods, circumstances and the opinions of your family or friends. Remember, your hope is built on Jesus Christ, the visible picture of the invisible God, and on the unchanging Word of God.

Walking into the Scriptures

Read John 1:12

Receiving Jesus

1. How does a person receive Jesus Christ?

2. When you received Jesus Christ, what did you become?

3. The name "Jesus" means "the Lord saves." Does the meaning of Jesus' name give you assurance that you are saved? If so, why?

Read 1 John 5:10–12

Life or No Life

1. What kind of life are we speaking of in this passage?

2. Who gives life?

3. Who has life?

4. Who does not have life?

Read Ephesians 2:8–10

Receiving versus Earning

1. How have you been saved?

2. How significant are your works in your salvation?

3. Whose workmanship are you and how were you created?

4. What is the expectation God has for those that He saves?

Read John 3:16–18

The Miniature Gospel

1. What did God love?

2. Who did God give?

3. Who will not perish?

4. How does "condemnation" fit into the discussion of these verses?

Read Romans 6:23

Wages

1. How does Romans 6:23 validate the statement, "Sin pays"?

2. What is the "gift" in this verse?

3. Through whom does this gift come? (Note: It's a *person.*)

Walking It into My Life

1. Someone has defined GRACE with this acrostic:
   God's
   Riches
   At
   Christ's
   Expense

How is this acrostic definition justified based on Ephesians 2:8-10?

2. Acts 1:8 tells us that we are witnesses for Jesus Christ. Every Christian should be able to briefly give a testimony of his or her faith experience. The apostle Paul gives a pattern to follow in the first chapter of First Corinthians. Write your own testimony using this pattern:

   a. Your life before being saved—"Brothers, think of what you were when you were called" (1:26).

   b. Your salvation experience—"It is because of him [God] that you are in Christ Jesus" (1:30).

c. What God is now doing in your life—"Therefore, as it is written: 'Let him who boasts boast in the Lord' " (1:31).

Walking a Little Deeper

Many people think that they can earn salvation through good works. Take a sheet of paper and fold it in half. On one side write the heading "CREDITS." List everything about you that you believe would please God. Now write the heading "DEFICIENCIES" on the other side. List things about you that you believe would displease God.

Review your two lists. Compare them to what Paul said in the passage you read. Then write in large letters over your credits the word "INSUFFICIENT." Over your deficiencies write the word "FORGIVEN." Take a moment to thank your gracious heavenly Father that your eternal life does not depend on you or anything about you but rests solely on your faith in the finished work of Jesus Christ.

Endnote

[1] Robert Cook, *Now That I Believe* (Chicago: Moody Press, 1975), 13.

STUDY TWO

Studying the Scriptures

The compass is an important tool for those who walk and hike in the mountains. Its purpose is to show direction. Even without landmarks, people who possess a compass can always find true north and can, therefore, always know where they are standing in relationship to the fundamental point of reference.

The Bible is a compass; it tells readers where they stand and it points them in the right direction. Composed of the Old Testament (thirty-nine books) and the New Testament (twenty-seven books), the Bible, often described as the Word of God or the Scriptures, is a manual for living. God has revealed Himself, His plan to save us from sin and His guidelines for living in the pages of this sacred and holy book.

The Bible is an inspired book. Its author is God, not men. This truth is confirmed in Second Peter, "For prophecy never had its origin in the will of man, but men spoke from God as they were carried along by the Holy Spirit" (1:21). When you study the Scriptures, you fill your mind with the very thoughts of

God. You have the advantage of God's counsel and wisdom. Through the Scriptures you will understand His plan for your life and receive light for living.

The Bible enables its students to escape the life of defeat and to embrace the victorious and fruitful life. On the flyleaf of an old Bible were inscribed these words: "Sin will keep me from this book, or this book will keep me from sin." The Bible provides salvation, safety and security for all who will explore its pages and dig up its treasures.

Walking into the Scriptures

Read Psalm 119:9–11, 105

A Devotional on the Word of God

1. According to this psalm, how can a young man keep his life pure?

2. What is the writer's request in verse 10?

3. What is the purpose of "hiding" God's Word in your heart?

4. Turn to verse 105. What two analogies are used for the Word of God?

Read Joshua 1:6–8

Commands to Joshua

1. What was Joshua to be careful to obey?

2. What would make Joshua successful wherever he went?

3. How often was Joshua to meditate on the Word of God?

4. What does this passage say about the necessity of daily Bible reading?

Read 2 Timothy 3:16–17

The Value of Scripture

1. How much of Scripture is God-breathed?

STUDY TWO

2. What four benefits are derived from Scripture?

3. What is the result of these benefits in the life of a believer?

Read Matthew 4:1–11

A Weapon against Temptation

1. Who led Jesus into the wilderness to be tempted by the devil?

2. How many times was Jesus tempted in this encounter?

3. How many times did Jesus use Scripture to overcome temptation?

4. Where did these Scriptures come from? (Your Bible may include a note in the margin that tells you.)

Walking It into My Life

1. Memorize Psalm 119:11. Check here when completed. ☐

2. In Study One, "The Assurance of Salvation," you learned that the Christian experience involves a personal relationship with Jesus Christ. Good relationships depend so much on effective communication. The Bible is God's way of communicating with you. Read Psalm 138:2 and Isaiah 66:2 and then write a brief statement concerning what they say about your relationship to God and His Word.

3. There are three steps to studying the Bible:

    a. OBSERVATION = What does it say?
    b. INTERPRETATION = What does it mean?
    c. APPLICATION = How does it apply to my life?

Over the next seven days read the following psalms and ask yourself the above three questions:

    ___ Psalm 1   ___ Psalm 42
    ___ Psalm 23   ___ Psalm 46
    ___ Psalm 34   ___ Psalm 51
    ___ Psalm 37

Write down your answers to the three questions for each psalm. If you have trouble coming up with

18 STUDY TWO

answers, ask an older Christian for help. Put an "X" by each psalm when you have read and studied it.

Walking a Little Deeper

At a time of great personal persecution Martin Luther wrote, "My conscience is captive to the Word of God. I cannot and I will not recant anything, for to go against conscience is neither right nor safe. Here I stand. I cannot do otherwise. God help me. Amen."[1]

Identify an area of potential struggle for you—perhaps a sin you are prone to or a responsibility you have trouble fulfilling. What does the Word of God say about it as compared to what the world says? (Use your concordance to find Scripture that speaks to your need.)

Where should you place your confidence and why?

What steps might you need to take to overcome this struggle?

Endnote

[1] Tim Dowley, ed. *Eerdman's Handbook to the History of Christianity* (Grand Rapids, MI: Eerdman's, 1977), 364.

STUDY THREE

Prayer

In an effort to inflate their worth, people often mention stars, dignitaries or celebrities that they have talked to personally. "I spoke to the Vice-President, or to the Most Valuable Player in the Super Bowl, to Miss America . . ." The Christian has the distinct honor of communicating with Someone who transcends all others, a Person who can be reached any place, any time, and who understands every piece of information that is given to Him—namely, the heavenly Father. This communication with God is called prayer.

Prayer is *indispensable* in the life of a believer. It is as critical as fuel to an engine, ammunition to a weapon or air to the lungs. John Bunyan wrote: "You can do more than pray, after you have prayed, but you cannot do more than pray until you have prayed."[1]

The richest encyclopedia on the practice of prayer is found in the life and ministry of Jesus Christ. Fifteen of His prayers are recorded in the Gospels. He prays at the beginning of His ministry and during His crucifixion. He prays early in the morning and late at night. He prays with joyful thanksgiving before a miracle and with painful agony in Gethsemane's Garden.

If Jesus found prayer so effective and so necessary, can His followers diminish its frequency and prominence in Christian living? The poet Tennyson made this stunning assessment: "More things are wrought by prayer than this world dreams of."[2] The biblical record and the history of the Church confirms it!

For this study, the following definition of prayer is understood:

> Prayer is a conversation between God and a person.

Walking into the Scriptures

Read Luke 11:1

"Teach Us to Pray"

1. What prompted one of Jesus' disciples to ask, "Teach us to pray"?

2. What does Luke 11:1 tell us about prayer?

Read Matthew 6:9-13

3. Jesus gave His followers a pattern for prayer in Matthew 6:9-13. It is best known as "The Lord's Prayer" but also has been called "The Model Prayer" or "The Disciples' Prayer." What six requests are listed in the prayer? (Hint: The first is not as much a request as a statement of fact.)

    a.

    b.

    c.

    d.

    e.

    f.

4. What does the beginning of the prayer say about the manner in which we approach God in prayer?

Read James 1:6-7

Principles of Prayer

1. What does James 1:6–7 say about the importance of having faith when we pray?

Read John 16:24

2. In ancient times, an individual's "name" represented his entire person, including his position and authority. What do you think it means to ask in Jesus' name?

Read Psalm 66:18 and James 4:3

Hindrances to Prayer

3. What are the two hindrances to prayer mentioned in these verses?

Walking It into My Life

1. As Christians we need to be a people of prayer. Prayer is a key to developing a close relationship with our God. We need to *regularly* and *consistently* pray. Yet prayer does not need to be complex or burdensome. For the next week do the following exercise:

   a. Identify a time when you have five to ten minutes alone. This could be first thing in the morning, at lunchtime or in the evening.

b. Start by quieting yourself before the Lord and acknowledging that God is your Father.
c. Each time write a one sentence prayer for a specific need.
d. Commit each and every need before the Lord.
e. At the end of the week note how God has changed and/or used you. Praise Him for answers received.

2. Just as prayer is a conversation between God and you, so reading the Bible is the primary way God talks to us. Slowly read Psalm 1 during your prayer time and pray a verse or portion of the psalm back to God. Then thank Him for speaking to you through His Word and for the privilege of being able to have a conversation with Him.

3. Sometimes we find it hard to get started in prayer. One useful tool for developing a sound, biblical style of prayer is to pattern our prayers after the way godly people prayed. We learn much by way of imitation. Three Old Testament prayers that use the same pattern can be found in Ezra 9, Nehemiah 9 and Daniel 9. From these examples we can develop a couple of useful acrostic models for prayer:

      A (adoration)   P (praise)
      C (confession) *or* R (repentance)
      T (thanksgiving)   A (asking for others)
      S (supplication)   Y (yourself)

(*Supplication* means making a request of God.)

24 STUDY THREE

Write a prayer using one of these acrostic models. Memorize the acrostic models and use them when you pray.

Walking a Little Deeper

1. How is prayer defined? Here are a few examples:

The ancients defined prayer as a "climbing up of the heart" unto God. —Martin Luther

Prayer is an approach to God, a pleading with God, an asking of God. —E.M. Bounds

Prayer is the one hand with which we grasp the invisible. —Andrew Murray

The hand of the child touches the arm of the Father and moves the wheels of the universe. —A.B. Simpson

Write your own definition of prayer:

2. Many Christians have made reference to the familiar axiom, "Prayer changes things." Prayer also changes people, and frequently those who are praying become the answer! Jesus asked His disciples to pray that the Lord of the harvest would send out laborers. Notice that later the Twelve were the ones sent out (see Matthew 9:37–10:5).

List three needs for which you are currently praying and identify how God might use you to answer them.

Prayer Need	"Sending" You
1._____	_____
2._____	_____
3._____	_____

3. We need to remember that our prayers must be in God's will. Imagine that a child came to you asking for something. List three requests a child could make that rightly would be answered "no."

What might you ask of your heavenly Father that He would rightly say "no?"

26 STUDY THREE

Endnotes

1 John Bunyan, "Quotation," *Tabletalk,* Vol. 2, No. 1 (Feburary 1987): 5.

2 Alfred, Lord Tennyson, *The Passing of Arthur,* l. 414.

STUDY FOUR

Witnessing

What would you think of someone who discovered the cure for cancer and kept it hidden away in a secret notebook? The thought of someone permitting others to experience unnecessary pain and loss is extremely troublesome. So, too, it would be tragic to keep the gospel to ourselves. Think of how grateful you are to the person or persons who introduced you to Jesus Christ and started you on the adventure of the Christian life.

Witnessing is a normal and natural activity for everyone who has embraced Jesus Christ. He is the good news that overcomes bad news, the cure for the cancer of the soul, the light that chases away the darkness, the companion who conquers loneliness. To witness is to speak through your lips and through your lifestyle the message that Jesus is the answer. This good news concerning Jesus Christ was to be distributed to the entire population of the planet. Jesus said as much in Acts 1:8:

STUDY FOUR

But you will receive power when the Holy Spirit comes on you; and you will be my witnesses in Jerusalem, and in all Judea and Samaria, and to the ends of the earth.

Every believer has the privilege and responsibility of participating in *evangelism*—sharing the good news of Jesus Christ with the world. Your circle of influence may reach across the street or across the sea, depending upon where the heavenly Father plants you and the opportunities He provides for you.

How many individuals will you talk to today? How many individuals will watch your actions or reactions today? These groups comprise your mission field. Jesus has brought you into His family and He intends that you participate in the grand plan of salvation by pointing others to Himself and His heavenly Father. Christianity was never to be a movement led by "a silent majority." You can know the joy of witnessing to people who are lost—people whose lives are fragmented and futile without faith in Jesus Christ.

Walking into the Scriptures

Read Matthew 4:18–20

Fishers of Men

1. What were Peter and Andrew doing when Jesus saw them, and why were they involved in this activity?

2. What did Jesus promise to make them?

3. What did Jesus ask Peter and Andrew to do?

Read Matthew 5:14–16

Lights

1. What is the purpose of light?

2. How are believers like a lamp on a lampstand or a city on a hill?

3. Where is your light to shine?

4. Give two reasons why your light should shine.

Read 1 John 1:1–4

Defining a Witness

1. Which of the five senses does John mention regarding his relationship with Jesus Christ?

2. Compose a definition of witnessing from verse 3.

3. Why did John and others proclaim Jesus Christ?

4. What emotion did John experience because he had written about Jesus?

WITNESSING 31

Read Acts 16:25-34

A Case Study

1. What were Paul and Silas doing at midnight?

2. What caused the jailer to wake up?

3. What question did the jailer ask Paul and Silas?

4. What answer did the two men supply?

5. Who else was affected by this witnessing encounter?

STUDY FOUR

6. What was the jailer filled with and why?

Walking It into My Life

1. In Study Three you learned about prayer. You now realize that your prayers must be in God's will. Do you believe it to be God's will that everyone should have an opportunity to respond to the gospel? Think about people you know that do not know Jesus as their personal Savior and Lord. Add them to your prayer list and pray regularly for their salvation. Pray that you might have the opportunity to be God's witness to them and that you may be able to lead one or more of these people to the Lord.

I will pray for the salvation of:

2. Our lives, as well as what we say, play an important role in our witness. On a separate sheet of paper list five things about your life that would be a positive witness for the Lord. For example, you may take criticism well on the job or you may not find it necessary to "get back" at someone who mistreats you.

Now list three things in your life that might be considered a negative witness for the Lord. For example, using language that would be inappropriate or losing your temper with your spouse or children.

Praise the Lord for those areas that are positive. Ask Him to work in your life to correct those areas that are a negative witness.

3. Invite someone you know to an event where the gospel will be presented. This could be a church service, a Christian concert, an evangelistic Bible study or a Bible-based seminar. Check this box when you have completed this assignment. ☐

Walking a Little Deeper

1. Every believer should be able to express the gospel clearly, simply and with gentleness and respect. One tool among many that has been found to be useful when leading someone to Jesus Christ is called the "Roman Road." Look up the Scriptures which are to be shared at each point of destination on the Roman Road.

   a. WHO has sinned?
      Romans 3:23
      Romans 3:10

   b. WHAT is the penalty of sin?
      Romans 6:23
      Romans 1:18

   c. HOW may I be saved?
      Romans 10:9-10

STUDY FOUR

   d. WHAT HAPPENS when I ask Christ to save me?

        Romans 10:13

Now mark each of these verses in your Bible for ready reference. Ask God to give you opportunities to share them.

2. In Study One, "The Assurance of Salvation," you wrote out your testimony. Before the next session share your testimony with at least one other person. Be prepared to report back on what happened.

3. How we treat people can be a powerful witness for the Lord. Identify an individual or family that has a specific need. It may be a material, financial or emotional need. Find a way to help meet that need in the name of Christ. What impact do you think this had on the individual or family? What impact did being Christ's witness have on you?

STUDY FIVE

Worship and Fellowship

The story is told of a man who disagreed with D.L. Moody on the importance of corporate worship (many people coming together in one place to glorify the Lord). This individual contended that he could worship God quite well on his own. A fire was burning in the room where the conversation was being held. Moody went to the fire and removed one log from the others. They watched as the log lost its bright orange hue and eventually burned out. The man understood the point. Anyone can worship God privately, but there is a special dynamic which emerges when God is worshiped in community.

The Bible provides many illustrations of corporate worship. The Israelites in the wilderness worshiped in and around the tabernacle, a movable church which accommodated a people on the go. Later the temple provided a central place where believers could gather in a permanent setting to interact with the Lord.

In the New Testament the early Church congregations worshiped in homes. They created opportunities for fellowship through such activities as prayer groups and feasts.

The strong impact of the first Christians upon their society can be largely attributed to their emphasis on worship and fellowship. It is imperative that today's disciples realize that we cannot go very far on the road of faith, or grow very much, without worship and fellowship. The Church works like a body, one part with many members, each member contributing to the health of the whole unit. Group worship and fellowship are two healthy exercises of the body of Christ.

Walking into the Scriptures

Read Psalm 29:2 and Revelation 4:11

Defining Worship

1. In Psalm 29:2 what is to be ascribed to the Lord?

2. What is God worthy to receive according to Revelation 4:11?

3. How is God described in these two verses which distinguishes Him from people?

Read Psalm 100

Joyful Worship

1. What are some of the words in this psalm which relate to celebration?

2. What descriptions distinguish God from mankind in these verses?

3. Who is to be involved in this joyful worship?

Read Hebrews 10:25

The Value of Worship

1. What is the habit of some people?

2. What is one particular advantage associated with assembling?

3. The "Day" in this verse refers to the return of the Lord Jesus to receive His bride, the people of His Church. What should the expectation of Jesus' return cause us to do?

Read Acts 2:42–47

Believers in Fellowship

1. To what were these believers devoted?

WORSHIP AND FELLOWSHIP 39

2. What did the believers have in common?

3. Where did these believers meet for worship and fellowship?

4. What were some of the results from the group worship and fellowship that was practiced in the early Church?

Walking It into My Life

1. One way of ascribing worth is through praise. The Psalms have much to say concerning praising our God. Using Psalm 146–150 and Psalm 100, begin your daily devotional time with God by reading one of these psalms each day, praising God in prayer and then listening quietly before Him.

Psalm 146	Done ___	Psalm 149	Done ___
Psalm 147	Done ___	Psalm 150	Done ___
Psalm 148	Done ___	Psalm 100	Done ___

40 STUDY FIVE

2. Many times we evaluate worship based upon what we get out of it rather than on what we put into it. Remember, the corporate worship service is a time when believers come together to unite in ascribing worth to our great God. Evaluate your participation in the next worship service you attend by answering these questions.

   a. Did I glorify God?

   b. Did I worship sincerely, with my whole heart?

   c. Did I encourage a visitor?

3. To experience good Christian fellowship the Bible tells us there are a number of things we are to do one to another. Identify them below and ask yourself when was the last time you did this.

Galatians 5:13

Colossians 3:13

Ephesians 4:2

Ephesians 5:21

I Thessalonians 5:11

Walking a Little Deeper

The Greek word *koinonia* is used to define fellowship, both between God and people, as well as between people. Explore what the following Scriptures teach about *koinonia*.

2 Corinthians 6:14

Galatians 2:9

Philippians 3:10

1 Corinthians 15:33

1 Peter 4:13

1 John 1:7

STUDY SIX

Stewardship

Stewardship pertains to the care and use of property entrusted to an individual. It extends to the moment of accountability when the owner evaluates how successfully the steward managed that which was assigned to him.

The Bible is very clear on the issue of ownership. Psalm 24:1 declares, "The earth is the LORD's, and everything in it, the world, and all who live in it."

It is crucial to understand that stewardship is an act of worship. Often the issue of giving a tithe (one-tenth of our income) and offerings beyond the tithe is relegated to secondary status. This is not biblical. How we respond to God in the area of giving speaks volumes about our love for Him and our degree of obedience to His Word.

Andrew Murray wrote, "The world asks, 'What does a man own?' Christ asks, 'How does a man use it?'" D.L. Moody remarked, "Tell me how a man spends his money and I will tell you what kind of man he is."

STUDY SIX

There is a direct correlation between our giving patterns and the depth and breath of our faith in God's ability to provide. When we give to the work of the kingdom, a partnership is formed with God. He has commanded that we give, and He has promised to provide.

Walking into the Scriptures

Read Proverbs 3:9–10

Firstfruits

1. Who is to be honored?

2. How is He honored?

3. If the Lord is honored, what two outcomes are projected in these verses?

Read Malachi 3:8–10

Tithing

1. How do we rob God?

2. Who was under a curse?

3. Where is the tithe to be brought?

4. What is the promise for those who tithe?

Read Matthew 6:19–21

Treasure

1. What happens to earthly treasures?

46 STUDY SIX

2. Where is treasure to be stored?

3. When you locate your treasure, what will you find there?

Read 2 Corinthians 9:6–8

How to Give

1. What is the law of sowing and reaping?

2. Who should give?

3. Where and how should the giving decision be made?

4. What kind of giver does God love?

5. What does God promise?

Walking It into My Life

1. How would you define being a good steward?

2. Most of us go to our dentist for regular checkups or take our car to the mechanic for periodic tune-ups. Our financial stewardship may also benefit from a periodic checkbook checkup. Review your checkbook to see where you have spent your money the past several months. What percentage went to kingdom work, how much to the needs of your family, how much to help those in need, how much was wasted?

If you have never put together a family budget, do so before the next time you meet. You can get a simple budget planning guide at your local Christian bookstore.

3. Since God is the all-wise owner of all we possess, we should seek His guidance in how we use the resources He has entrusted to us. Make a list of the significant resource decisions you expect to make in the next six to twelve months. Your list may include such decisions as buying a car or a house, your level of giving to missions, choosing a public or private school for your children and/or the type of vacation you plan to take. Now bring these listed items before God on a regular basis to truly seek His will for you as His steward. Share these items with one or two others who can pray with you and for you.

Walking a Little Deeper

1. Stewardship is first and foremost a spiritual issue. All Jesus spoke about tithing is in Matthew 23:23 and Luke 18:12. What do these verses say about a self-righteous approach to tithing?

2. What does First John 3:17–18 say about giving to others who are in need?

3. In Luke 21:1–4 Jesus commends a specific example of giving. What can you learn from this example and apply to your life?

**Walking with the Word
Bible Studies**

LEADER'S GUIDE

Foundations is a discipleship course for believers. It is designed to develop in the follower of Jesus Christ an understanding and application of core values which are essential for dynamic Christian living.

The study guide in the beginning of this book asks students to look up specific Scriptures and to fill in answers to the questions based on those verses. It also includes sections on "Walking It into My Life" to help students apply what they have studied to their daily lives. The "Walking a Little Deeper" section is for those students who want to tackle a little more challenging material.

Foundations is designed so that it can be used in Sunday school classes, small groups or for individual study. It contains six lessons. You may choose to do one lesson a week or spend two weeks on each lesson.

This Leader's Guide provides answers and additional background material (in italics) for most of the questions in the study guide. If you are going through this study on your own, the Leader's Guide can be used if you are stuck on a question or would like more information on the things you are learning.

If you are leading a group study, the Leader's Guide includes suggestions (also in italics) to help you keep the discussion on track. It is intended to help you guide the group; it should not be seen as an "answer key" that limits group discussion. Keep in mind that the new believers in your group are looking to you as an example. Determine to be approachable, open and honest. In so doing they will be more likely to share areas where they are struggling.

As you lead the group, remember Jesus' words in Matthew 28:19–20: "Therefore go and make disciples of all nations, baptizing them in the name of the Father and of the Son and of the Holy Spirit, and teaching them to obey everything I have commanded you. And surely I am with you always, to the very end of the age."

Foundations is one more disciple-making tool which, if studied and applied, will facilitate teaching which leads to obedience.

STUDY ONE
The Assurance of Salvation

Walking into the Scriptures

Read John 1:12

Receiving Jesus

1. How does a person receive Jesus Christ?

Believe in His name. (You may want to share your experience of receiving Jesus Christ. When and how did you come to believe in Him? On the other hand, you may want to wait until later in the lesson when the students are invited to share their testimonies.)

2. When you received Jesus Christ, what did you become?

A child of God. Read Romans 8:15–18. When we were saved, we received the Spirit of sonship, or adoption, that enables us to call God "Abba" (Aramaic for "Daddy"). The use of this term confirms that we have a close, personal relationship with the Father through Jesus Christ.

3. The name "Jesus" means "the Lord saves." Does the meaning of Jesus' name give you assurance that you are saved? If so, why?

His name communicates His primary reason for coming into the world.

Read 1 John 5:10–12

Life or No Life

1. What kind of life are we speaking of in this passage?

Eternal life. (You might want to read Jesus' words to Martha that He spoke at the tomb of Lazarus in John 11:25–26.)

2. Who gives life?
God.

3. Who has life?

He who has the Son—that is, anyone who believes in Christ. (Beyond the promise of eternal life, talk about how "life in his Son" begins now—how as "a new creation; the old has gone, the new has come," as it says in Second Corinthians 5:17.)

4. Who does not have life?

He who does not have the Son. (Stop and pray for family and friends of group members who have not yet chosen life in Christ. Ask the Lord to fill each person in the group with such deep assurance of his or her salvation that his or her joy will be contagious.)

Read Ephesians 2:8–10

Receiving versus Earning

1. How have you been saved?

Our salvation is based on the fact that Jesus Christ paid the penalty for our sins on the cross. We receive this salvation by faith—by simply believing that Christ died for us. Sometimes we may feel that faith is somehow unreal. Paul Little has commented that faith is a common occurrence in our lives; for ex-

ample, we might open a can of soup, heat it and eat it without any particular thought as to whether it would be safe to do so.[1] Why? We have a degree of faith that it will be wholesome and not harmful.

(Ask the group to name things they deal with on a daily basis as an expression of faith. For example, that other drivers will stop at a red light, that the pilot really knows how to fly, that our car will go the way we steer it. Talk about how much more assured we can be of our salvation since the object of our faith is God Himself. All other objects are temporal and imperfect; God is eternal and absolutely perfect.)

2. How significant are your works in your salvation?
Our works cannot save us. If we could work hard enough to gain our salvation, it would no longer be a free gift. (You might also want to look up Titus 3:5 and talk about His mercy that saved us while we were yet sinners.)

3. Whose workmanship are you and how were you created?
We are God's workmanship, created in Christ Jesus. Someone has said, "God doesn't make junk." Be aware that there may be some individuals in your group who have been wounded deeply and, as a result, still have difficulty seeing themselves through God's eyes. Encourage each person to rejoice in his or her uniqueness and the special plan God has for him or her.

4. What is the expectation God has for those that He saves?
That they will do "good works." Challenge group members to think about specific good works God may desire to see accomplished through their lives. And encourage them to take the limits off God. "[He] is able to do immeasurably more than all we ask or imagine" (Ephesians 3:20).

Read John 3:16–18

The Miniature Gospel

John 3:16 has been labeled "The Miniature Gospel" because

it condenses the good news of salvation. It has been used to lead people to Jesus Christ more than any other verse in the Bible. The two verses that follow it are very helpful in understanding the thrust of John 3:16.

1. What did God love?
The world.

2. Who did God give?
His Son, Jesus Christ.

3. Who will not perish?
Whoever believes in Him.

4. How does "condemnation" fit into the discussion of these verses?
God's intent was to save the world—not condemn it. Those who believe are not under condemnation (see Romans 8:1). Those who do not believe are already condemned.

Read Romans 6:23

Wages

1. How does Romans 6:23 validate the statement, "Sin pays"?
Sin does pay wages: "The wages of sin is death." In addition to the eternal consequences, talk about the immediate consequences of sin; for instance, how sexual immorality might result in an unplanned pregnancy, a sexually transmitted disease, and/or a failed marriage.

2. What is the "gift" in this verse?
Eternal life.

3. Through whom does this gift come? (Note: It's a *person*.)
Christ Jesus our Lord.

54 FOUNDATIONS

Walking It into My Life

1. Someone has defined GRACE with this acrostic:
   God's
   Riches
   At
   Christ's
   Expense

How is this acrostic definition justified based on Ephesians 2:8–10?
It is a gift of God, not anything we could do for ourselves. It required a dear price, the blood of Jesus Christ. (You might want to read to the group Philippians 2:6–8 for a deeper understanding of all Christ willingly sacrificed for our salvation.)

2. *(Invite those who want to share the testimony they have written to do so. If you have not already done so, this would be a good point at which to share your own salvation story.)*

Walking a Little Deeper

In the exercise listing "credits and "deficiencies," some of the "credits" a person might come up with include being good to one's family, trying to do right, going to church, etc. "Deficiencies" might include such things as getting angry easily, cheating on income taxes, selfishness, etc. (Do not ask anyone to share the items on their lists, but be encouraging if someone does. Read the apostle Paul's account of his "credits" in Philippians 3:4-9, and consider his new assessment of them.)

(Ask the group how they felt as they listed their credits and wrote the word "insufficient," as they listed their deficiencies and wrote "forgiven." Close by inviting sentence prayers of thanksgiving for the gift of God's grace.)

STUDY TWO
Studying the Scriptures

(To introduce this session, you may want to read the story below which illustrates the value of knowing the Scriptures.)

John Calvin Reid shares this short exchange which occurred between a passenger on a Mississippi steamboat and a riverboat captain.

"Captain," said the passenger to the pilot, "I suppose you know every sandbar in the river."

"No," replied the captain, "as a matter of fact I know where only a few of the sandbars are."

"But if you don't know where the shoals and shallows are located, how can you pilot your boat?"

The captain answered, "Why should I go . . . hunting for the sandbars? I know where the deep channel is."

(Talk about how we do not have to know every aspect of the river of life; we just have to know where the channel is located. If we want to safely navigate in life, we need to study the Bible! Ask the Lord to speak to each member of the group through His Word as you begin today's study.)

Walking into the Scriptures

Read Psalm 119:9–11, 105

A Devotional on the Word of God

Psalm 119 is the longest of the psalms (176 verses). It is divided into twenty-two stanzas, each one beginning with a different letter of the Hebrew alphabet (there are twenty-two letters). There are eight different Hebrew words which are used for the Word of God. In our English translation words such as laws, statutes, commandments, decrees and promises represent these words. Every stanza uses at least six different words and

56 FOUNDATIONS

some stanzas use all eight. If you read the whole psalm, you will harvest a significant understanding of the power and authority that is found in God's Word.

1. According to this psalm, how can a young man keep his life pure?
By using God's Word as the guide for his decisions.

2. What is the writer's request in verse 10?
Don't let me stray or be detoured from God's commands.

3. What is the purpose of "hiding" God's Word in your heart?
So that a person will not sin against God. (Talk about some ways that we can hide God's Word in our hearts, such as learning Scripture choruses, following Scripture memorization plans, reading and re-reading verses of Scripture that speak to specific needs and writing them out. Encourage the group to memorize Psalm 119:11.)

4. Turn to verse 105. What two analogies are used for the Word of God?
A lamp which gives light (truth); a light that illuminates the way we should walk.

Read Joshua 1:6–8

Commands to Joshua

After the death of Moses, Joshua was God's handpicked successor to lead the people of Israel.

1. What was Joshua to be careful to obey?
All the law that Moses gave.

2. What would make Joshua successful wherever he went?
If he would not veer from the law.

3. How often was Joshua to meditate on the Word of God?
Day and night.

4. What does this passage say about the necessity of daily Bible reading?

The discipline of daily reading and meditation on the Scriptures is essential, not incidental, to righteousness and a holy lifestyle.

Read 2 Timothy 3:16–17

The Value of Scriptures

1. How much of Scripture is God-breathed?

All of it! (Read Hebrews 4:12 and explain to the group that because the Bible was authored by God the Holy Spirit, it is living and active—it is real and pertinent to your life.)

Some people have the idea that the Bible is written in some sort of secret code, understandable only to "experts." This is absolutely untrue, but we do need to realize that it takes time and effort to study the Scriptures. As A. Morgan Derham said, "The Bible is not like a slot machine. If you put in [only] five minutes' reading time, you don't necessarily get a 'blessing' (or anything else) out of it." And Robert A. Cook adds, "The Bible . . . becomes of value to you when you get hold of it for yourself. Never leave a passage of Scripture until it has said something to you."

2. What four benefits are derived from Scripture?

Teaching, rebuking, correcting and training in righteousness. (Be prepared to give an example of how a specific Scripture has impacted your life in one of these ways.)

3. What is the result of these benefits in the life of a believer?

They are "equipped for every good work." The Bible gives us the right "equipment" to live a Christian life.

Read Matthew 4:1–11

A Weapon against Temptation

1. Who led Jesus into the wilderness to be tempted by the devil?

The Holy Spirit. (You might want to read Hebrews 2:18 and

4:15. Because Jesus experienced temptation, He understands the temptations we face. Talk about the example He has given us of how to handle temptation.

2. How many times was Jesus tempted in this encounter?
   Three times.

3. How many times did Jesus use Scripture to overcome temptation?
   Three times.

4. Where did these Scriptures come from?
   Deuteronomy 8:3; 6:16; 6:13. Memorizing Scripture can help in fighting temptation. The more Scripture you study and memorize, the more you have to fight with.

Walking It into My Life

1. Memorize Psalm 119:1.
   (Ask if anyone was able to memorize the passage; be careful not to embarrass anyone who was not able to do it. Be sure you have memorized the passage yourself—there is no more powerful teaching tool than a good example!)

2. Read Psalm 138:2 and Isaiah 66:2 and then write a brief statement concerning what they say about your relationship to God and His Word.
   Your statements might read something like this:
   Psalm 138:2—God and His Word are preeminent. I am humbled before God and His holy Word.
   Isaiah 66:2—God thinks highly of those who respect His Word.

Read the following quote from Dr. Billy Graham.

> God caused the Bible to be written for the express purpose of revealing to man God's plan for redemption. God caused this book to be written that He might make His

everlasting laws clear to His children, and that they might have His great wisdom to guide them and His great love to comfort them as they make their way through life.[2]

3. Ask members of the group to share what they discovered as they read Psalm 1. For example:

What does it say? *There are differences between righteous men and wicked men, both in how they lead their lives and the outcome of their lives.*

What does it mean? *A person should take heed of the life he or she leads. Are they following that which is evil and wicked, or are they following that which is righteous as found in the Word of God? The Lord is watching and He will judge.*

How does it apply to my life? *I need to be in the Word more to be better able to discern right from wrong in the eyes of God.*

Encourage the group to make daily Bible reading a habit and to begin their Bible study time with a brief time of prayer, seeking the Holy Spirit's ministry for their study.

Walking a Little Deeper

Identify an area of potential struggle for you. What does the Word of God say about it as compared to what the world says?

(This is a good discussion question. Some of your students may need help identifying an appropriate passage of Scripture. Be prepared to share from your own experience how the Word of God is helping you in your struggles.)

Where should you place your confidence and why?

We should always place our confidence in the truth. God's Word is the truth.

What steps might you need to take to overcome your struggle?

Submit to the Word of God, seek counsel and prayer support from another Christian, praise God for His promises.

Re-read God's promise in Second Timothy 3:16–17 and close in prayer thanking Him for the provision He has made for us through His Word.

60 FOUNDATIONS

STUDY THREE
Prayer

Walking into the Scriptures

Read Luke 11:1

"Teach Us to Pray"

1. What prompted one of Jesus' disciples to ask, "Teach us to pray?"
   Jesus' example. Just as His disciples were strongly influenced by His example, we can be an example to those around us.

2. What does Luke 11:1 tell us about prayer?
   It can be learned.

Matthew 6:9–13

3. Jesus gave His followers a pattern for prayer in Matthew 6:9-13. It is best known as "The Lord's Prayer" but also has been called "The Model Prayer" or "The Disciples' Prayer." What six requests are listed in the prayer? (Hint: The first is not as much a request as a statement of faith.)
   a. *"hallowed be your name"*
   b. *"your kingdom come"*
   c. *"your will be done"*
   d. *"give us today our daily bread"*
   e. *"forgive us our debts"*
   f. *"lead us not into temptation, but deliver us from the evil one"*

(Point out that the first three are God-related and the last three are man-related.)

The Lord's Prayer is designed to serve as a teaching instrument in the development of a believer's conversational skills with God the Father. Jesus' pattern of prayer is very similar to the style of Jewish Rabbis. G. Campbell Morgan observed: "The Jewish Rabbis taught the people what were known as 'index prayers.' These consisted of a collection of brief sentences, each one of which suggested a subject of prayer."[3]

4. What does the beginning of the prayer say about the manner in which we approach God in prayer?

As Christians, we can approach God, our heavenly Father, in prayer as children who are loved would approach their loving earthly father. He wants to hear from us and to give us good gifts. Jesus said, "If you, then, though you are evil, know how to give good gifts to your children, how much more will your Father in heaven give good gifts to those who ask him!" (Matthew 7:11).

Read James 1:6–7

Principles of Prayer

1. What does James 1:6–7 say about the importance of having faith when we pray?

It is essential.

E.M. Bounds, a great man of prayer and faith, remarked:

The possibilities of prayer are the possibilities of faith. Prayer and faith are Siamese twins. One heart animates them both. Faith is always praying and praying is always believing. Faith must have a tongue by which it can speak. Prayer is the tongue of faith. Faith must receive. Prayer is the hand of faith stretched out to receive. Prayer must rise and soar. Faith must give prayer the wings to fly and soar. Prayer must have an audience with God. Faith opens the door, and access and audience are given. Prayer asks. Faith lays its hand on the thing asked for.[4]

Read John 16:24

2. What do you think it means to ask in Jesus' name?

Calling upon the name of a person was considered the same as calling upon the person—everything they represented and possessed. When someone came in "the name of the king," it was as if the king were present. When we ask in "the name of Jesus," we are asking on behalf of the King of kings.

Read Psalm 66:18 and James 4:3

Hindrances to Prayer

3. What are the two hindrances to prayer mentioned in these verses?

a. We must not "cherish sin" in our heart. (Ask the group what they think this means.)

b. Asking with wrong motives. (Talk about how subtle this is, how easy it is to fool ourselves and justify our motives.)

Walking It into My Life

1. *(Invite group members to share how their prayer lives have grown this past week as a result of the suggestions in the study guide. If anyone has brought the one-sentence prayers he or she wrote, invite him or her to share them with the group.)*

It is very important to develop a habit of regular and consistent prayer. Many believers find it helpful to choose a specific time every day to pray—a time when they are least likely to be interrupted. Remember, Satan will do whatever he can to keep you from developing a closer walk with God.

Even Jesus needed time to be alone with His Father. (Read Matthew 14:23, Mark 1:35 and Luke 5:16.) Prayer was a priority in Jesus' life. We need to follow His example, and make it a priority in our lives as well.

2. *(Invite members of the group to share how they used their Bibles in their prayer time.)*

Using the Bible in prayer can be very rewarding. For example, after reading Psalm 1, you could pray that you would delight in God's Word and not walk, stand or sit with sinners or sinful activities. (Have the group open their Bibles to Psalm 1 and show them how you turned the first few verses of the psalm into a prayer.)

(Close the session by thanking God for speaking to you through His Word and for the privilege of being able to have a conversation with Him.)

LEADER'S GUIDE 63

3. Write a prayer using one of the acrostic models.

(Invite members to share their written prayers. You may want to read aloud one of these prayers from Ezra 9, Nehemiah 9 or Daniel 9 asking the group to identify the various parts of the prayer. Then ask, "What percent of the prayer is adoration/praise, confession/repentance and thanksgiving/supplication?" Discuss how these estimates compare to their own prayer lives. Have a time of prayer using the ACTS or PRAY acrostic as a pattern. Ask for a volunteer for each of the four parts of the prayer. Encourage them to memorize these acrostic models and to use them in their own prayer lives.)

Walking a Little Deeper

1. How is prayer defined? . . . Write your own definition of prayer.

(Talk about the definitions given. Invite members of the group to share the definitions they have written. Then look again at the definition given in this study guide: "Prayer is a conversation between God and man.")

(If you have time and the group expresses interest, you may want to explore one or more of the following areas.)

- How often should we pray? *See Psalm 55:17; Daniel 6:10; Ephesians 6:18.*
- How long should we pray? *See Matthew 6:7–8; 15:25; Luke 6:12; 18:13; 23:42.*
- What is the best position for prayer? *See 1 Samuel 1:26; 2 Samuel 7:18; Ephesians 3:14; Ezekiel 3:23.*

2. List three needs for which you are currently praying and identify how God might use you to answer them.

(Be prepared to help launch this discussion by sharing a need you are aware of and how God might want to use you to help meet this need.)

64 FOUNDATIONS

3. List three requests a child could make that rightly would be answered "no."
- *To have something that would be harmful to him or her, such as playing with matches.*
- *To be permitted to do something beyond the known rules, such as staying out past curfew or charging an item on his or her parents' credit card without permission.*
- *To do something that is clearly a violation of God's Word, such as being involved with satanic games and/or activities or not attending worship services on the Lord's Day.*

What might you ask of your heavenly Father that He would rightly say "no"?

To seek His blessing for something that is contrary to His commands, like cheating on your taxes.

STUDY FOUR
Witnessing

(Begin this session with prayer, thanking the Lord for the privilege of being His witness. Ask Him to make each person sensitive to the needs of people around him or her and ready to share his or her faith through the power of the Holy Spirit.)

Walking into the Scriptures

Read Matthew 4:18–20

Fishers of Men

1. What were Peter and Andrew doing when Jesus saw them, and why were they involved in this activity?

They were fishing, because they were professional fishermen.

2. What did Jesus promise to make them?

Fishers of men.

LEADER'S GUIDE 65

3. What did Jesus ask Peter and Andrew to do?
"Follow me."

Read Matthew 5:14–16

Lights

1. What is the purpose of light?
Provide illumination . . . overcome darkness.

2. How are believers like a lamp on a lampstand or a city on a hill?
They are hard to hide, easy to see.

3. Where is your light to shine?
Before men. (Talk about places where it is not easy to let our light shine.)

4. Give two reasons why your light should shine?
It is God's intent that people may see the difference Christ is making in your life and give praise to God. (You may want to read what Paul wrote in the opening chapter of his letter to the Romans: "I am not ashamed of the gospel, because it is the power of God for the salvation of everyone who believes" [1:16].) Also, God knows that we will shine the brightest when we take our eyes off ourselves and place them on others and on their needs.

Read 1 John 1:1–4

Defining a Witness

John, one of the twelve apostles who witnessed the ministry of Jesus up close and personal, wrote this letter. He also wrote the Gospel of John, Revelation and Second and Third John.

1. Which of the five senses does John mention regarding his relationship with Jesus Christ?
Hearing, seeing, touching.

2. Compose a definition of witnessing from verse 3.
Witnessing is telling others what you have experienced first-hand.

3. Why did John and others proclaim Jesus Christ?
So that others may join the circle of Christian fellowship and have fellowship with the Father and His Son, Jesus.

4. What emotion did John experience because he had written about Jesus?
Even as John experienced joy in writing about Jesus, one of the greatest joys we can experience is sharing our faith with others.

Read Acts 16:25–34

A Case Study

After being stripped and beaten for a crime they did not commit, Paul and Silas were thrown into prison. The jailer was told to guard them carefully. Taking no chances, he threw them into the inner cell and fastened their feet in stocks.

1. What were Paul and Silas doing at midnight?
Praying and singing hymns to God was certainly not a normal response to the physical pain they must have been experiencing and to the predicament they were in. It was no secret that many who were thrown in prison never came out alive.

2. What caused the jailer to wake up?
A violent earthquake

3. What question did the jailer ask Paul and Silas?
"What must I do to be saved?"

4. What answer did the two men supply?
Believe in the Lord Jesus.

5. Who else was affected by this witnessing encounter?
All the jailer's family (They were baptized). Even as Paul and

LEADER'S GUIDE 67

Silas' witness extended to the jailer's family, our witness may touch more lives than we expect.

6. What was the jailer filled with and why?
He was filled with joy because he and his whole family had come to believe in God.

Walking It into My Life

1. In Study Three you learned about prayer. You now realize that your prayers must be in God's will. Do you believe it to be God's will that everyone should have an opportunity to respond to the gospel?
Yes! (Refer to Matthew 28:19, the Great Commission. Jesus commands His disciples to go to all nations, meaning every people group of the world. While we may never leave this country, we can help to send missionaries. And we can be a missionary right here at home. Remind them to pray regularly for the people they added to their prayer list who do not know Jesus as their personal Savior and Lord. And stop and pray right now that God will enable them to lead one or more of these people to the Lord.)

2. On a separate sheet of paper list five things about your life that would be a positive witness for the Lord. . . . Now list three things in your life that might be considered a negative witness for the Lord.
(In response to the list they made, you might want to set up a system of accountability between you and your group members. Invite them to share one or two areas where they struggle. Read Philippians 1:4–6. Assure them that God will complete the good work He has begun in them. Pray for them regularly and follow up periodically. Always attempt to encourage them rather than be critical.)

3. Invite someone you know to an event where the gospel will be presented.
Help your group members to identify events.

Walking a Little Deeper

1. Look up the Scriptures which are to shared at each point of destination on the Roman Road.
(You might want to role play the Roman Road experience one or more times. Encourage them to memorize these key verses. If they memorize one for each session, in the span of six sessions the entire Roman Road could be mastered.)
Most likely, very few people you witness to will be won to Jesus Christ on the first encounter. It is comparable to a baseball game: A batter hits a single and moves the runner from first base to second base. The next batter may move the runner from second base to third. Finally, another batter may send the runner home! In witnessing you may not always score the run, but your witness may move the runner closer to home. Ask the group if they can think of other analogies.
Consider this quote from Dr. John Stott:

> The New Testament does not always mention whether the Word which was evangelized was believed, or whether the inhabitants of the towns and villages evangelized were converted. In biblical usage, to evangelize does not mean to win converts, but simply to announce the good news irrespective of results.[5]

(Close by reading First Corinthians 3:5-9 and thanking God for the part He calls each one of us to have in bringing others to the saving knowledge of Jesus Christ.)

2. In Study One, "The Assurance of Salvation," you wrote out your testimony as an exercise. Before the next session share your testimony with at least one other person. Be prepared to report back on what happened.
(Ask if anyone shared his or her testimony. How did he or she feel prior to sharing this testimony? What was the individual's response? How does he or she feel about sharing his or her testimony in the future? Encourage your group members by

telling them about one or more of your attempts at witnessing that you felt was "less than effective.")

Jesus can use each of us, no matter how stumbling and awkward we may feel our words are, to spread the good news. You don't need to become a theologian to be a witness for Christ. As disciples we are responsible only to be witnesses. God, the Holy Spirit, convicts of sin (see John 16:8) and provides salvation.

3. Identify an individual or family that has a specific need. . . . Find a way to help meet that need in the name of Christ. What impact do you think this had on the individual or family? What impact did being Christ's witness have on you?

(Encourage them to consider ways they can be a witness through helping to meet someone's need.)

STUDY FIVE
Worship and Fellowship

(Ask the group how last week went. Do they see change in areas of their lives where they have not felt they were making a positive witness? Remind them again that God will complete the good work He has begun in them.)

Walking into the Scriptures

Read Psalm 29:2 and Revelation 4:11

Defining Worship

The word "worship," or a form of the word, occurs in the Bible over 200 times. Worship means "to ascribe worth" or to "give God that of which He is worthy." The two Scriptures above reinforce this idea of worship as "giving worth" or "affirming worth."

1. In Psalm 29:2 what is to be ascribed to the Lord?
The glory due His name.

70 FOUNDATIONS

2. What is God worthy to receive according to Revelation 4:11?
Glory and honor and power.

3. How is God described in these two verses which distinguishes Him from people?
He has a worthy name. He is holy. He is the Creator.

Read Psalm 100

Joyful Worship

1. What are some of the words in this Psalm which relate to celebration?
Joy, gladness, joyful, thanksgiving, praise, thanks

2. What descriptions distinguish God from mankind in these verses?
He is the maker . . . we are the made (v. 3).
He is the Shepherd . . . we are the sheep (v. 3).
He is good (v. 5).
He exhibits eternal love (v. 5).
He is faithful throughout all generations (v. 5).

3. Who is to be involved in this joyful worship?
All the earth.

Read Hebrews 10:25

The Value of Worship

1. What is the habit of some people?
They have stopped meeting together. (Talk about the importance of being aware of who is missing from Sunday morning worship and reaching out to them. Knowing that they were missed and that someone cares can make a huge difference to them.)

2. What is one particular advantage associated with assembling?
It provides opportunity for encouragement. (You might want

LEADER'S GUIDE 71

to discuss some hindrances to giving and receiving encouragement: rushing out of church, busyness, superficiality, etc. Suggest that they make a commitment to give specific encouragement to at least one person each Sunday morning.)

3. The "Day" in this verse refers to the return of the Lord Jesus to receive His bride, the people of His Church. What should the expectation of Jesus' return cause us to do?

Meet together more frequently. (Tying back to last week's study on witnessing, talk about the responsibility and privilege we have to share our testimonies with others especially in light of this verse. Sometimes the first step is simply inviting someone to an event where the gospel will be presented. Ask if anyone did this assignment from last week.)

Read Acts 2:42–47

Believers in Fellowship

1. To what were these believers devoted?

To the apostles' teaching, fellowship, breaking of bread, prayers.

2. What did the believers have in common?

Everything. (Although most of today's believers do not sell all their possessions and hold everything in common, what are some other things, besides possessions, we can hold in common? To launch this discussion read Galatians 6:2. How can we "carry each other's burdens"?)

3. Where did these believers meet for worship and fellowship?

In the temple courts and in homes. (Encourage your group to seek and create opportunities for worship and fellowship outside the church walls. Suggest that before the next session they invite a person or couple to have fellowship with them. Identify some areas of conversation that would enable them to get to know one another better. After this time of fellowship, evaluate how they came closer to the person and then to God. What would they do differently next time? Discuss how the nature of

72 FOUNDATIONS

the conversation went. Who controlled the conversation? Would Jesus Christ have felt welcome in their fellowship? Should they have had a time of prayer?)

4. What were some of the results from the group worship and fellowship that was practiced in the early Church?
  Everyone was filled with awe (v. 43), many wonders and signs (v. 43), glad and sincere hearts (v. 46), praising God (v. 47), enjoyed the favor of the people (v. 47), people were getting saved on a regular basis (v. 47).

Walking It into My Life

1. *(Talk about the assignment in the study guide to begin each day's devotional time by reading a psalm and praising God. How did completing this exercise affect their worship experience? Encourage them to come to their daily quiet time and Sunday morning worship with a heart and mind that is prepared for an encounter with the living God.)*

2. *(Talk about how focusing on their participation in corporate worship, rather than on what they got out of it, changed their experience.)*

3. To experience good Christian fellowship the Bible tells us there are a number of things we are to do one to another. Identify them below and ask yourself when was the last time you did these things.

Galatians 5:13	*Serve one another.*
Colossians 3:13	*Forgive one another.*
Ephesians 4:2	*Bear with one another.*
Ephesians 5:21	*Submit to one another.*
1 Thessalonians 5:11	*Encourage one another.*

Read Romans 12:4–5 and talk about how each believer has an interdependent role to play in the body of Christ.

Walking a Little Deeper

1. The Greek word *koinonia* is used to define fellowship, both between God and people, as well as between people. Explore what the following Scriptures teach about *koinonia*.

Koinonia, as it was used in the Greek and Hellenistic world, meant unbroken fellowship between God and humans or the bond between people. Fellowship had a vertical thrust (divine—human) and also a horizontal thrust (human—human). Worship furnished an opportunity for fellowship in both a vertical and a horizontal direction.

2 Corinthians 6:14—*A believer should not be linked to a nonbeliever.*
Galatians 2:9—*Fellowship should bring about agreement and cooperation.*
Philippians 3:10—*We identify in the sufferings of Christ when we fellowship with Him.*
1 Corinthians 15:33—*All believers need to fellowship regularly with like-minded believers. Spending too much time with non-believers will have an impact on our Christian walk. We are commanded to go and make disciples, but we must be sure we are not being impacted by the evil of this world. (Discuss how to deal with this issue.)*
1 Peter 4:13—*We can rejoice in the fellowship we have with Christ.*
1 John 1:7—*We fellowship with Christ and other believers when we walk in the light.*

(Close the session by thanking God for the way His Word really does give us the light we need for our daily walk and our relationships with others. Ask that He will help each group member to make worship a daily priority and that He also will help him or her to strengthen his or her relationships with other believers.)

STUDY SIX
Stewardship

The authentic Christian views money and resources with a different perspective. A.W. Tozer wrote:

> It is one of the glories of the Christian religion that faith and love can transmute lower values into higher ones. Earthly possessions can be turned into heavenly treasures. . . .
>
> As base a thing as money often is, it yet can be transmuted into heavenly treasure. It can be converted into food for the hungry and clothing for the poor; it can keep a missionary actively winning lost men to the light of the gospel and thus transmute itself into heavenly values.[6]

(As you begin this session, ask the Lord to reveal to you and each participant His heart regarding stewardship issues.)

Walking into the Scriptures

Read Proverbs 3:9–10

Firstfruits

God demands first place in our lives. The stewardship area is no different; His expectation is the first and best. The Old Testament spoke of the firstfruits (the earliest pickings) of the harvest and the best lamb of the flock, one without blemish or spot.

1. Who is to be honored?
   The Lord.

2. How is He honored?
   With the wealth and firstfruits of all crops. (Talk about what the "firstfruits" might be for twentieth-century Christians.)

3. If the Lord is honored, what two outcomes are projected in these verses?
Barns filled to overflowing, vats brim over with new wine. (See Philippians 4:19.)

Read Malachi 3:8–10

Tithing

1. How do we rob God?
In tithes and offerings. (You might want to read Psalm 89:11 which asserts God's ownership. Then share the following story.)

> Bishop Edwin Hughes preached a sermon on stewardship in which he told the congregation that man is only a tenant and everything belonged to God. That afternoon a farmer showed the preacher his fields and then said, "I have the deed to that land. Does it belong to me?" The Bishop answered, "Ask me again one hundred years from now." The bishop made his point; because we are only on this earth for a short time, can we really say we "own" anything?[7]

2. Who was under a curse?
The whole nation.

3. Where is the tithe to be brought?
The storehouse. (Explain that today, we think of our "storehouse" as the place where we are fed spiritually—our local church.)

4. What is the promise for those who tithe?
God will open the floodgates and pour out blessings. (This may be a good opportunity to share how this has proved true in your life.)

Read Matthew 6:19-21

Treasure

1. What happens to earthly treasures?
Moth and rust destroy them. Thieves steal them.

2. Where is treasure to be stored?
In heaven. (Ask how, specifically, can we store up treasures in heaven.)

3. When you locate your treasure, what will you find there?
Your heart. (Ask the group to bow their heads and close their eyes for a few minutes to examine their own lives. Ask them to spend a few moments thinking on these questions: Where is your heart? Do things matter more to you than relationships? More to you than the Lord?)

Read 2 Corinthians 9:6-8

How to Give

1. What is the law of sowing and reaping?
Sow sparingly, reap sparingly; sow generously, reap generously. (You might want to turn to Jesus' parable of the sower in the beginning of Matthew 13. Ask the group to think of illustrations of this principle. For instance, when a child gives his time and attention halfheartedly to a school subject, he will not learn all he can from that class.)

2. Who should give?
"Each man"—in other words, everyone. (Note that this applies to all believers, regardless of income.)

3. Where and how should the giving decision be made?
In his heart. (This might be a good point to talk about the importance of not comparing what we give with what another believer gives. We each need to search our own hearts and give "not reluctantly or under compulsion.")

4. What kind of giver does God love?

A cheerful giver. (Ask the group how they would feel about accepting a gift that was not given willingly and joyfully.)

5. What does God promise?

All grace will abound to you, you will have all you need and you will abound in every good work.

Consider the following quote from A.B. Simpson, founder of The Christian and Missionary Alliance: "What is grace? Grace is something given us, something we get, not something we give. God does not require us to give as though it was a difficult exercise. He wants to give us the spirit of giving."[8]

Walking It into My Life

1. How would you define being a good steward?

(Help the group to see that stewardship involves more than just how we handle our finances. Talk about things like time and talents to help them understand the spiritual nature of stewardship. As in every other area of life, blessings result from dealing with the practical issues of life from the spiritual perspective; problems result from failing to do so.)

2. *(Ask the group what they learned from their "checkbook checkup." Ask if anyone worked on a family budget in the past week. Share some of the lessons you have learned in the area of stewardship, budgeting, etc., and stress the priorities of God and His kingdom first, family next, the needy third.)*

3. *(Invite the members of the group to share their lists of resource decisions and be ready to pray with them about it, but do not press the issue. For some, such a list may be too private to share.)*

Walking a Little Deeper

1. All Jesus spoke about tithing is in Matthew 23:23 and Luke 18:12. What do these verses say about a self-righteous approach to tithing?
While Jesus endorses tithing, He is critical of motivation that is self-righteous. Self-righteous activities are not pleasing God.

2. What does First John 3:17–18 say about giving to others who are in need?
(Talk about needs in your community. Are they being met? Is there something the Lord would have you or your church do?)

3. In Luke 21:1–4 Jesus commends a specific example of giving. What can we learn from this example and apply to our lives?
The widow gave out of her poverty while the rich gave out of their surplus. Jesus commands that our giving should affect our lifestyle. We must do more than give out of our surplus.

Billy Graham has said that identifying ourselves with Christ "demands a daily recognition of His lordship and a willingness to put Christ ahead of every pursuit of life." [9]

(Close the session by inviting anyone who would like to pray aloud to do so.)

Endnotes

[1] Paul E. Little, *How to Give Away Your Faith* (Downer's Grove, IL: InterVarsity Press, 1966), 105.
[2] Billy Graham, *Peace with God* (Dallas, TX: Word Publishing, 1984), 24.
[3] G. Campbell Morgan, *The Practice of Prayer* (New York: Fleming H. Revell, 1906), 66.
[4] E.M. Bounds, *The Possiblities of Prayer* (Grand Rapids, MI: Baker Book House, 1979), 34-35.
[5] John Stott, *Christian Mission in the Modern World* (Downer's Grove, IL: InterVarsity, 1975), 38.

6 A.W. Tozer, *The Alliance Witness,* October 8, 1958.
7 Charles L. Allen, *Prayer Changes Things* (Westwood, NJ: Revell, 1964), 77.
8 A.B. Simpson, *Missionary Messages* (Camp Hill, PA: Christian Publications, Inc.), 97.
9 Billy Graham Evangelistic Association, *Studies in Discipleship* (Minneapolis, MN: BGEA, 1976), 1.

The sequel to this book, *Foundations II*, includes lessons on the following topics:

The Lordship of Jesus Christ
The Holy Spirit
The Will of God
Suffering and Healing
Missions
The Second Coming